The Cockatoo Dictionary

A Poor Choice Of Words

Tom Klingenfuss

IVEUGWQMCSIOK.XLIKW
FOYZLXUSPEJNJXUIOUBT
QDAYCUMUDWSJDQLBW
SGHOFHRYX.

Abodessors- *Plural Noun*

[ah-boe-dess-ers] people who believe that men should act like women and women should act like men.

Example: The amount of abodessors within western civilization is resulting in men crying in public and women telling people to suck their dicks.

Annodane- *Noun*

[ahn-noe-daen]
a dog whose owners
have not properly trained
the pet, therefore making
the dog a complete
nuisance to be around.

Example: Every time an
annodane runs up to me
in a park I feel like it's
within my right to kick
the stupid mut.

Apogenitives- *Plural Noun*

[ah-poe-jehn-ih-tihvs] vegans who constantly tell the people they meet that they are vegans.

Example: Apogenitives are the holy rollers of people on special diets.

Appascear- *Noun*
[ahp-puh-skair]
the unofficial dress code
for the people you see
when you shop at
Walmart.

Example: It seems like
every time I shop at
Walmart the appascear is
getting more and more
disturbing.

Arduartam- *Noun*
[ar-doo-ore-tum]
a genius that is a tradesman, a geneticist and an inventor with multiple patents.

Example: The man I met was more than just your ordinary plumber. The man I met was an arduartam!

Audackema- *Noun*
[awe-dah-keh-muh]
is the defective human
being who thinks that it's
ok to talk in theaters
while the movie is on.

Example: Every time I sit
near an audackema at
the cinema, I begin to
have murderous urges
that I have to quell for
two hours.

Begalsaners- *Plural Noun*
[beh-gawl-sih-ners]
lies that people tell each other under the guise of being kind while the truth would be more beneficial, regardless of hurt feelings.

Example: Husbands generally use begalsaners every time their wives ask them if they look fat in a dress.

Busukit- *Noun*

[buh-soo-kiht]

an individual or company that rapidly creates new products that lack quality due to the speedy production process. This is oftentimes due to a lack of integrity in pursuit of quick money.

Example: Cartoon Mouse Studios is a busukit!

Camortine- *Noun*
[cah-more-teen]
a dog that that has lived considerably longer than it should have lived. The dog is typically around 18 years-old and might be blind with no control over its bladder.

Example: I always felt sad as a child when it was time to take the family camortine to the vet for the final sleep.

Cavling- *Noun*

[cahv-leeng]

a man that breaks girls' hearts by his mere existence. God is the only person to blame (or thank, depending on one's perspective).

Example: One of the requirements for an actor to become James Bond is that he has to be a cavling.

Cosillace- *Noun*
[coe-sihl-ihs]
a room where the air conditioning is so bone chillingly cold that a person can get sick from the temperature if they don't wear extra layers.

Example: The doctor's office was such a cosillace that you'd think you were in a morgue.

Crimtasterpomps-

Plural Noun

[crihm-tah-ster-pumps] educators that take part in indoctrinating minors, in K-12 schools, that the only way to be successful in life is to go to college and accrue an obnoxious amount of debt, for a degree that has little to no value and a poor return on investment, without even calculating in the minimum of four years of opportunity costs.

Example: The public school system is littered with crimtasterpomps!

Dantelek- *Noun*
[dahn-tehl-ehk]
is that no good troublemaking neighbor that will tattletale to the city if there's the smallest infraction to report.

Example: The new neighbor made the mistake of parking five inches in front of the dantelek's driveway.

Debosise- *Verb*
[deh-boe-size]
is when a feminist shames another woman for losing weight because "they were already beautiful," supposedly.

Example: Adele is probably the most famous woman to be debosised.

Detaliot- *Noun*
[deh-tah-lee-uht]
a person who encourages mentally ill people to believe in the delusions that they experience.

Example: The detaliot being interviewed on the morning show said that children who believe they have five arms and twenty-five fingers should be affirmed in that belief.

Dillucant- *Noun*
[dihl-loo-kent]
a person who believes
that they are smart
solely based upon the
fact that they have a
college degree.

Example: The dillucant
with a master's degree in
gender studies is almost
never the smartest
person in the room.

Dimeltune- *Noun*
[dih-mehl-toon]
a song that was popular at the time of its release, but is not popular in the years that follow.

Example: Every so often I hear a dimeltune that came out when I was in high school.

Dimeral- *Verb*
[dih-mer-awl]
the action where someone dials the same wrong number multiple times.

Example: The other day a guy named Toby dimeraled me four times in one hour.

Disceptiot- *Noun*
[dih-sep-tee-uht]
an imbecile that can't tell the difference between someone joking and someone being serious.

Example: Becky was such a disceptiot that she insisted on finding out who's chicken I was talking about when I asked her, "Why did the chicken cross the road?"

Duplisweet- *Noun*
[doo-plih-sweet]
a synonym for cinnamon.
That's all duplisweet is, a
synonym for cinnamon.

Example: I added
duplisweet to my oatmeal
this morning.

Edesmals– *Plural Noun*
[eh-dehz-mahls]
dog treats that smell like they would be delicious if humans were to eat them.

Example: I'm always tempted to try the edesmals my dog gets for Christmas each year.

Empalnon- *Noun*
[ihm-pahl-nawn]
a fictional idea concocted
by someone's
imagination that the
general public believes to
be a part of factual based
reality.

Example: Global warming
is an empalnon that
people shouldn't worry
about. Climate change is
a very serious matter
though.

Evidature- *Noun*
[eh-vih-duh-chur]
a double standard that exists because of the natural order of the world.

Example: The evidature of women being considered sluts and men being considered studs in regards to sexual promiscuity is as old as history itself.

Fablivant- *Noun*
[fah-blih-vent]
a person that has a
warped sense of reality
as a result of being a
compulsive liar.

Example: The young
fablivant thought that he
might be a good lawyer
someday. He also
thought that the sun
rises in the west.

Fasumate- *Verb*
[fah-sue-mate]
the action of gaining copious amounts of weight shortly after getting married.

Example: Becky began to fasumate two weeks after her honeymoon.

Fetromonia- *Noun*

[feh-troh-moe-nee-uh]
the trend of straight
women marrying other
straight women due to
not finding a man to
marry.

Example: Fetromonia is
becoming more common
amongst millennials
within the last decade.

Filadepts- *Plural Noun*

[fihl-uh-dehps]

parents that can't keep their children under control in public places and therefore are a detriment to the good order of society.

Example: Filadepts that let their kids run around screaming in the grocery store should have their parent cards revoked for gross negligence.

Fimbeliot- *Noun*
[fihm-behl-ee-uht]
a child who is old enough to know that Santa Claus isn't real, and yet somehow still believes that Santa is real. This child is far from being the smartest kid in class.

Example: The poor fimbeliot told his classmates that they would get coal in their stockings if they didn't stop saying that Santa Claus wasn't real.

Flawokens- *Plural Noun*
[fluh-woe-kehns]
men that are weak of mind, body and spirit. These are men that fathers would never want their daughters to marry.

Example: Flawokens need to man up and work on exercising and self-improvement to become capable men.

Franisters- *Plural Noun*
[frah-nih-sters]
nerds and geeks who talk crap about video game consoles like they're still living in the nineties.

Example: The franisters were arguing about the current console war in the game store.

Gadoller- *Noun*

[guh-dawl-er]
this is the "bad" videogame controller that contributes to a guy losing a game against his friends.

Example: Billy lost to Bobby at smash because he had the gadoller.

Gafferationists-

Plural Noun

[gah-fur-aye-shun-ists] gamers who ungratefully whine and complain about how video game creators could have done better with a game or anniversary collection.

Example: All the gafferationists were upset when Super Mario 3D All-Stars didn't contain Super Mario Galaxy 2.

Garspound- *Verb*

[gar-spoond]
is when retards pontificate about complete nonsense. It should be noted that when I say, "retards," I am not referring to the mentally challenged. I'm referring to the retards who get Master's Degrees in gender studies and other poppycock.

Example: My professor would oftentimes garspound about how proud he was that the child of his XY chromosome sibling was a wormself.

Gasager- *Noun*

[gah-sah-jur]

in regards to marriage, a girl that should cash in on her looks in her younger years, because she has no personality or mind to fall back on in her later years.

Example: Becky always talked about how she wanted to marry a man that loved her for who she was as a person and not for her looks. Unfortunately for Becky, she was in fact a gasager.

Gobsurded- *Adjective*

[gawb-ser-did] something so unbelievably moronic, that the cacophony of driveling noises from an infant seem intelligible in comparison.

Example: I, Tom Klingenfuss, created the word "gobsurded" in an attempt to describe the Season 1 Finale of *The Rings of Power*.

Grosingerate- *Verb*
[groe-sihn-jer-iht]
is when a psychologist
misdiagnoses a young
boy with ADHD because
he's acting like a young
boy.

Example: In the nineties
it was common for
psychologists to
grosingerate lively grade
school boys.

Helener- *Noun*

[hel-lin-er]

a woman that men would risk their lives to go to war over in order to protect her. It should be noted that there are considerably less heleners since the advent of radical feminism.

Example: Unlike a sandberschumer, a helener is the type of woman that men would die for.

Idejennial- *Noun*

[ih-deh-jeh-nee-uhls]
a person that cannot tell you what a man is or what a woman is. It should be noted that some of these gobsurded individuals can answer this simple question, but for some reason they won't.

Example: I used to sit next to an idejennial when I studied at university. I would always get an earful whenever I used a word with "man" in it because I was imposing blah, blah blah. I would always stop listening halfway through the first sentence.

Ignemotientals-

Plural Noun

[ihg-neh-moe-shun-uhls]
people who believe that
EQ, (emotional
intelligence), is a real
thing. These people are
sort of like children who
believe in Santa Claus,
except for the fact that
these people aren't
children, they're just
naive.

Example: Ignemotientals
rarely know that EQ is a
term that was created by a
journalist.

Jetarsist- *Noun*
[jeh-ter-ist]
a person who believes
that minorities are
incapable of being racist
because they're
minorities.

Example: It's always
annoying when a jetarist
says racist statements
with impunity.

Kamarkles- *Plural Noun*
[kuh-mar-kuls]
public figures that no one likes and everyone despises.

Example: Our country always regrets it when members of the royal family marry kamarkles.

Kandepeds- *Plural Noun*
[kahn-deh-pehds]
people who think that being on their feet all day at work in an airconditioned building is the equivalent to working out.

Example: Many kandepeds work as cashiers at grocery stores.

Kihortants- *Plural Noun*
[kih-hoar-tents]
people that cannot keep a plant alive no matter how hard they try. Somehow these people even manage to kill succulents.

Example: It is never a good idea for kihortants to work in greenhouses.

Kisectinates- *Plural Noun*
[kih-sec-teh-nets]
children that behave so
monstrously, that they
make men want to get
double vasectomies.

Example: Billy always
wanted to have children
someday, or at least he
did until he came across
some kisectinates at the
department store.

Labeter- *Noun*

[lah-beh-ter]

a man that complains about where he is in his life and what he is to society, but he doesn't make any effort to improve his situation.

Example: A labeter can easily be found on internet forums talking about how unfair his life is.

Lamortecation- *Noun*

[luh-more-tih-kae-shun]
the dissolution of western civilization via ideologies, ignoring scientific fact, ignoring objective reality, Christians and Christian churches not holding biblically based values and beliefs, a general lack of morality, revisionist history, sexual promiscuity, men being taught to act women and women being taught to act like men.

Example: The lamortecation in the United States can easily be found throughout every city in every state.

Laprogent- *Noun*
[lah-proe-jehnt]
a college degree that has little or no return on investment once the individual obtains the said degree.

Example: My gender studies professor actually makes a decent living despite having a laprogent.

Leramen- *Noun*
[lair-uh-mehn]
a women's haircut that is typically used by lesbians and is not considered a traditionally feminine haircut.

Example: One of the greatest talk show hosts of all time has a leramen.

Laskivan- *Noun*
[lah-skih-vahn]
a woman that doesn't have any of the basic homemaking skills that traditional wives and mothers possess, (which is fine nowadays, I guess).

Example: Modern-day men are finding that there are many laskivans amongst the ranks of modern-day women.

Loricide- *Noun*

[lore-ih-side]

an act of loricide occurs when a production company makes a movie/show adaptation of a literary work without respecting the source material. Loricide oftentimes results in a gobsurded adaptation that should be ridiculed by everyone.

Example: Amazon Prime is responsible for the loricide Professor Tolkien's literary masterpieces.

Maboval- *Noun*
[muh-boe-vawl]
a person that walks through life with a misplaced sense of superiority that makes others not want to engage with them unless it's absolutely necessary.

Example: Becky had maboval tendencies that made her lose many of her friends throughout her life.

Macravent- *Noun*
[mah-cruh-vent]
a type of coward that hides behind a text message when there's a difficult conversation to be had in person.

Example: Billy was always afraid of confrontations with other people. With that being said, it's no wonder that he was a macravent.

Malustench- *Noun*
[mal-oo-stench]
food that is unhealthy and lacks nutrition to the point that the food smells exactly like its digested form once it's in the toilet.

Example: My supervisor at work always ate malustench for lunch from the gas station. His favorite was the giant bean and cheese burrito.

Mecogyst- *Noun*
[meh-coh-jihst]
a person who makes most of their decisions based on their feelings whilst abandoning logic, reason and rationale.

Example: It's never a good idea to have a mecogyst in charge of any amount of people.

Miloatheners- *Plural Noun*
[mih-lowth-in-ers] millennials that despise the millennials that give the millennial generation a bad name.

Example: Many miloatheners despised receiving participation trophies after being on undefeated sports teams.

Minstrovine- *Noun*

[mihn-stroe-veen]
a child that acts like a
monster in public due to
a lack of discipline by
their parents.

Example: One time at the
grocery store I saw a
minstrovine tear open a
box of corn flakes and
scatter the contents
along the isle nine floor.

Miroganine- *Noun*
[mih-roe-jeh-nine]
a dog that is so ugly that humans sometimes find the animal to be cute or adorable.

Example: Pugs are one of the most desired breeds of miroganines around the world.

Nagapplent- *Noun*
[nuh-gahp-plehnt]
the guy in the friend group that everyone makes fun of. This guy is loved very much by his friends and for this reason he does not take offense when they make fun of him.

Example: Billy was the nagapplent whenever it was just us guys hanging out.

Nesanoron- *Noun*

[neh-sahn-ore-ohn]
a psychologist or therapist that needs help with their own mental health to the extent that they should not be treating others as a professional.

Example: I once knew a nesanoron that thought humans and buffalos were more or less the same creature.

Nofiast- *Noun*

[noe-fee-ist]

a business that prefers to push an ideology instead of making money.

Example: Several years ago, a razor company decided to become a nofiast in spite of their consumer base being mostly men.

Noraseur- *Noun*
[nore-uh-soor]
a man that says whatever the heck he wants to say regardless of whatever consequences may ensue.

Example: One of the greatest comedians of all time was a noraseur.

Norvientists- *Plural Nouns*

[nore-vihn-tihsts]
people who are considered bigots for acknowledging basic human biology as undeniable reality.

Example: Many independent news commentators on the internet are considered to be norvientists.

Nourifant- *Noun*
[noor-ih-fahnt]
an adult that is an extremely picky eater. There is reason to believe that nourifants are picky eaters because their parents never made them eat food they didn't like as children.

Example: I have a cousin that's a nourifant. He only eats sandwiches and combination pizza.

Ofantle- *Noun*

[oe-fahn-tul]

a piece of modern-day technology that used to be depicted as futuristic technology in old movies and television shows.

Example: A video call is an ofantle that used to seem impossible in the sixties.

Opafictionate- *Noun*
[oe-puh-fihk-shun-iht]
a person that believes in the mythical "oppressive patriarchy," that men of all ages are a part of in the past, present and future.

Example: One of my professors at university is a proud opafictionate who claims that she isn't married because she's a proud opafictionate. She also has short blue hair, piercings in weird places, and tattoos all over her body that is somehow shaped like a toad.

Pacluress- *Verb*

[pah-cler-ehs]

is when a girl does her makeup in such a poor fashion that she looks akin to a clown.

Example: Many girls pacluress their faces when first learning how to do their makeup.

Pathidler- *Noun*

[pah-thid-ler]
someone who is so ridiculously lazy, that the only endeavor the person puts effort into is how to be able to be even more lazy.

Example: My supervisor at work, the one who ate malustench every day, he was also pathidler.

Pefutate- *Verb*
[peh-few-tate]
is when an individual
defends an objectively
awful movie or show.

Example: Many of my
friends pefutate shows on
the Cartoon Mouse
Studios streaming
service.

Postircal- *Noun*
[poe-steer-kul]
a ridiculously unlikely play made in a sports game that will no doubt go down into sports history.

Example: The rookie professional basketball player made a postircal that was trending on the internet for over a week.

Prexlible- *Noun*

[prex-lih-buhl]

a completely poppycock excuse that is commonly used and accepted amongst the general population.

Example: Billy's favorite prexlible to use when asked for help is "I'm busy that day."

Quementicals-

Plural Noun

[kweh-mehn-tih-kuls]
women that believe it is okay behavior for them to get violent or break the law because of something their boyfriend or husband did.

Example: Most quementicals get visibly upset if you point out that their behavior is unacceptable.

Raserush- *Verb*

[rah-ser-ush]
the action where someone undercooks corned beef hash to the degree that it's a disgusting mush. It is a sin and people will keep doing it unless someone speaks up, or at the very least writes about it in a dictionary that was published in 2023.

Example: My great uncle used to raserush hash in the microwave.

Replexicant- *Noun*

[reh-plecks-ih-cant]
a girl that's trying to get rid of a guy who's talking to her, by giving one-word answers to his questions.

Example: Billy didn't notice that Becky was a replexicant and continued to ask her questions throughout the entire baseball game.

Reumalant- *Noun*
[roo-muh-lawnt]
a person that repeats opinions or talking points as fact without examining the validity of what they're saying. This person is likely unaware of whether or not what they're saying is true whilst firmly believing in what they said.

Example: I met many reumalants during the time I spent studying at university.

Sancrivate- *Noun*
[sahn-crih-viht]
a non-religious individual
that lives more like a
Christian than most
Christians.

Example: Susanne
thought Billy was a
Christian, but he turned
out to be a sancrivate.

Sandberschumer- *Noun*

[sand-bur-shoo-mer]
a woman that is the exact opposite of a helener. Men tolerate her existence and don't want to be around her at all because of her demeanor and jarring personality.

Example: Unlike a helener, a sandberschuumer is the type of woman that men would die to get away from.

Sansumerate- Noun
[sahn-soo-mur-iht]
a person that still
believes that legacy
media news stations tell
the truth without having
any bias.

Example: Many people of
the boomer generation
are also sansumerates.

Scrisage- *Noun*
[scrih-zidge]
the facial expression of a
woman when she has
marriage written all over
her face, oftentimes
occurring when she sees
a man that she desires.

Example: The young lady
had a look of scrisage
when she saw the man
walking by the foot of the
staircase.

Segmentuous- *Adjective*
[sehg-men-chew-us]
is used to describe a painstakingly long line at a grocery store that has no end in sight.

Example: There's a value store near the gym that always has a segmentuous line when I go shopping there.

Selidate- *Adjective*

[sel-uh-dit]

a word used to describe a person who treats their birthday like it's a federal holiday.

Example: One of my friends is a very selidate person, but I still like him anyway.

Sewerver- *Noun*

[soo-wer-ver]

a waiter or waitress that are complete trash at their job. They'll forget to serve someone their meal, then they'll get the meal incorrect, and then they'll serve the correct food not properly cooked. Basically, they seemingly fail at their job on every level.

Example: There is a De La Fiesta restaurant downtown that has a sewerver that is always working the lunch shift.

Shodifuls- *Plural Noun*
[shaw-dih-fools]
published academic papers
that have no objective
research and do not use
the scientific method and
are accepted as fact. To
be clear, these papers are
pretty much fantasy from
creative minds.

Example: Academia is
littered with shodifuls that
sometimes win awards for
their "groundbreaking"
discoveries.

Smirlus- *Noun*
[smer-lus]
the sound of the chorus of giggling a group of girls make, oftentimes occurring around a male they find attractive.

Example: He could tell by the smirlus surrounding the young lady that she meant business, and that he would have to start running instantly if he wanted a decent head start.

Spaterist- *Noun*
[spae-ter-ist]
a person that has a
visceral hatred of spiders
that burns with a hot
fiery passion deep within
the confines of their soul.

Example: My closest
friends are aware of the
fact that I am very proud
of being a rabid spaterist.

Stalmortion- *Noun*
[stahl-more-shun]
the fatigue a person gets when they spend too much time in Walmart. Those who suffer from stalmortion fantasize about going to the kitchen isle to kill themselves with a three-dollar butter knife.

Example: If I'm in a bad mood when I go to shop at Walmart, I almost always get a case of stalmortion. Luckily, I'm cured of stalmortion when I leave the store.

Swadoltem- *Noun*
[swah-doel-tuhm]
a product that people buy
even if they know that it
was made in part by child
labor. The product is that
good.

Example: I really like my
cell phone. I know that it
is a swadoltem, but I just
avoid thinking about that
minor detail and use it to
call people guilt free.

Tearismation- *Noun*

[tair-iz-mae-shun] occurs when a church focuses on making a spectacle out of Sunday morning services instead of focusing on the Bible.

Examples: I don't go to churches that engage in tearismation.

Tesch. aran- *Noun*
[tehs-cair-in]
a man that conducts
himself in a manner that
commands respect from
everyone who is around
him.

Example: Billy's older
brother is a tescharan
that can captivate a large
group of people when he
speaks about a subject
he's passionate about.

Texensate- *Verb*
[tecks-ihn-ate]
is when a production company preemptively makes excuses for why their movie or show will do so poorly both financially and popularity wise.

Example: Cartoon Mouse Studios almost always texensates the shows it puts out on it's streaming service.

Trallace- *Noun*

[trahl-es]

a lie that's so obvious and so poorly thought out, that a child wouldn't be fooled by it and might in fact be able to do better.

Example: Becky was caught off guard when she was asked to help out with a community service project, so she said the first trallace that came to mind.

Ufarsist- *Noun*

[oo-fair-sihst]
a phrase made up of words that are repeated in an attempt to sound wise.

Example: The most ridiculous ufarsist I ever heard was "value value."

Vacebol- *Noun*
[vah-see-bull]
a vaccine that does not prevent the infection or transmission of the disease it is designed to stop.

Example: In the year of our Lord 2021, a very popular vacebol was used by an extremely large group of people.

Vimarent- *Noun*
[vih-mair-ehnt]
a video game that is extremely bad. This game has bad design, poor functionality and isn't enjoyed by anyone.

Example: The Atari had many vimarents that were coming out like baby rabbits.

Wamulent- *Noun*
[wah-moo-lehnt]
a woman that has such unrealistic standards for a potential husband, that she will inevitably buy a dog and die alone.

Example: Wamulents are on the rise in North America and other places with similar cultures.

Wokehearted- *Adjective*
[woke-har-tid]
people who are wokehearted are fragile to the extent that they either break down or froth at the mouth whenever something politically incorrect is said or done.

Example: During my time studying at university, I met many wokehearted individuals that were affirmed in their beliefs by professors.

Xerafal- *Noun*
[zair-eh-fawl]
the worst possible wingman a guy could ever get.

Example: No man wants a xerafal for a friend. Once a man is determined to be a xerafal, he should hand in his bro card immediately.

Yaquarn- *Noun*
[yah-kwarn]
a bottled water brand that tastes unnatural to some and downright disgusting to others.

Example: I've always thought that Da**** is a Yaquarn.

Yumaloft- *Noun*
[yoo-muh-lawft]
an adult male with a very, very, very bad handshake. This flaccid fish handshake can prevent a man getting a job at an interview and can make women lose all attraction for the said man, and rightfully so.

Example: There is nothing more off-putting to my hand than that of shaking hands with a yumaloft.

Zanerus- *Noun*

[zae-ner-uhs]

a completely bogus call by a referee in a sporting event. It's the type of call that should get the referee fired.

Example: I remember watching a championship football game where a zanerus cost the red and gold team the trophy.

Zonfelates- *Plural Noun*
[zawn-fehl-ates]
cat owners that think cats are better pets than dogs.

Example: I have very few friends that are zonfelates. It should be noted that I became good friends with them before I found out that they were zonfelates.

Check out *Don't Shoot Me I'm Only The Joke Writer* on Amazon. It's the best jokebook of the whoring twenties!

Also check out the Cockatoo Digitals YouTube Channel as well as CockatooNews.com.